I0116974

Stag Night 2011

The Best Man's Guide To Organising Stag Weekends and Batchelor Parties

3rd Edition

First published in 2003
© Copyright 2003, 2006, 2010
Steve Emecz

The right of Steve Emecz to be identified as the author of this work has been asserted by him in accordance with Copyright, Designs and Patents Act 1998.

All rights reserved. No reproduction, copy or transmission of this publication may be made without written permission. No paragraph of this publication may be reproduced, copied or transmitted save with the written permission or in accordance with the provisions of the Copyright Act 1956 (as amended). Any person who does any unauthorised act in relation to this publication may be liable to criminal prosecution and civil claims for damage.

Paperback ISBN 9781907685095
eBook ISBN 9781907685101
Kindle/Mobipocket ISBN 9781907685118

Cover design by Staunch

Published by MX Publishing, London, England
335 Princess Park Manor, Royal Drive, N11 3GX

For.........every soon-to-be groom that has woken up tied to a lamp-post, painted green, left on an island or, in my case, with whip marks that took six weeks to heal.....................and the best men that put them there.

Introduction

So you are the Best Man. You have on your shoulders the daunting task of organising your best friend / brother's stag - making the delicate balance between ensuring he not only lives through it but actually enjoys it[1] while at the same time fulfilling all his mates' needs to see him humiliated for being stupid enough to get married.

The good news is that this is going to be fun. The bad news is that it will take a bit of organising and the challenge is that you will be dealing with a group of lads - we're generally crap at admin and you will spend a lot of time chasing around after your stag's lazy-arsed mates unless you make participation extremely easy. The first step is to make them feel part of the game so contact them early.

Remember its so much sweeter if the stag has absolutely no idea where he is going and what you will be doing. This also enables you to wind him up for weeks and weeks in advance. You must, must make the most of the wind up. It's worth splashing out on a classic stag movie to send to him in the run up – there's some listed in the back of the book. The Hangover was great, but there are some older films that are a bit more realistic which can be more un-nerving.

---

[1] Contrary to popular belief (and thousands of previous amateur examples) the groom should actually enjoy around 75% of his stag night.

Home vs Abroad

In a similar way to the rise of the 'staycation' (people holidaying at home) a straw poll of the recent stags has revealed that the home stag has strengthened in the last couple of years. A big factor here has been the increase in the cost of flights. Gone are the days when low cost flights could be had easily for £30. There is a section on low cost flights at the back that goes into more detail, and foreign destinations are by no means out of reach but we have beefed up our coverage of in-country stags this edition.

The Wonders of Facebook

You've got to love it. The first edition of Stag Night was a nightmare to research – back in 2003 broadband didn't exist and trying to research using the internet was pretty painful – every 2nd search ended up at a porn site (honest love, I am researching the book!).

For this 2010 edition we've set up a Facebook fan page for Stag Weekends and each new edition from now will contain information and stories posted by fans of Stag Weekends from around the world.

So as you read this remember that your exploits on your stag have a potential literary purpose – your pictures could be useful for generations of young men for centuries.

An Apology to Our American Cousins

Previous editions of Stag Night, much to my surprise, sold very well in America.

Most of the book, the ideas and stories transfer very well across the pond to the US but the travel locations are biased to stags from the UK. I'm not apologising for this, I'm a Brit and much as I pleaded with my wife to let me spend six months in the US 'experiencing' more batchelor parties in the cause of 'research' she wasn't having any of that – women eh? (as I type this I know I'm going to pay for that one).

So what I have tried to do is include the American word next to the English where I have used slang. I decided not to remove the slang – I'm not a complete sell-out, and besides I know you find it an endearing part of the British humour (or at least my American friends seem to find us talking like we're from the 1930s all the time amusing).

However, you need to know here that birds=ladies. To have put the translation next to that word would have taken ages.

You will have already guessed that Stag Night is the same as Batchelor Party, and Stag Weekend is basically a long Batchelor Party spread over an increasing number of days [my record personally is a 5 day 'stag weekend' in Ibiza].

Who, What, When, Where, How?

It is years since 'Stag Night' has transformed into 'Stag Weekend' and the choice is almost endless.

The very best way to start once you have the list of lads is to open up the question of where to go and what to do (even if you have already got it sorted in your own head) to the whole team.

These days this is easy to do on email. You will get some really poor ideas but you will also get some gems. You can piece these together but you will also learn some stuff about your stag that you didn't know. Try and answer the initial question:

Location versus Activity?

Is your stag more likely to enjoy a new and exciting place to get drunk or a more activity orientated stag?

Nail this one early as it will help you eliminate thousands of possibilities.

Budget

The next consideration is the dosh *(money).*

Opinion is divided on what is realistic and indeed fair to set as a budget for a stag weekend/night.

The following suggestions don't include drinking money – add £30 a night for that (unless you're in Eastern Europe then £15 should do....., or Paris £100 a night - ouch)

Under £100 – you need to be thinking on the lines of a 'night'

£150 – not bad for a weekend. This should cover accommodation and activities/flight.

£200+ - so you're stag has waited ages to get married and is already in his 30s and all his mates can afford to splash out.

£300+ - you can stretch to a couple of nights and a few extras as well.

This is always a tricky one to work out – once you have got a list from the stag then try and get an idea from a few of them what stage of life his mates are in. If they have all just started working and you suggest a flash weekend in New York then the take-up will be low.

Paying for Drinks

I know it takes effort but for god's sake use a whip (everyone gives you cash and you buy the drinks until the pot runs out – then repeat). The easiest way to split the group into little annoying cliques is for people to get into rounds with the people they know. You take charge and grab some wedge from each of them. This is also an easy way to ensure that the stag doesn't pay for any drinks.

If you are abroad, it may seem a little geeky but if you don't already have one, invest in a hidden wallet. Pickpockets are not stupid – they only have to see you hit the bar a couple of times to put two and two together. Losing your own drinking money is a sod – it's even less funny when multiplied by fifteen or so.....

Note: You'll have to abandon this if you go to a club as unless the place is shite and empty then you will have to fight to get to the bar and the group will have split up trying to pull anyway.

Dressing Up

Not for the lazy as this takes more effort but nothing attracts the ladies like a bunch of dressed-up guys. It's almost as if they assume we must have a sense of humour. If you are really bold then drag is a serious laugh but Vikings, Romans, Superheroes etc. are fairly easy to do and are that bit more interesting.

A really nice one spotted recently in New York was pinstripe suits, red ties, bowler hats and copies of the Financial Times.

Note: Make sure that the places you are going are well aware that you are coming kitted out. I've been part of a Viking party that turned up to a London club (where we had pre-arranged with the bouncer) only to be turned away as it was his night off and the new guys told us to sod off. Thumbs up to the Aussie Bar "The Outback" in Covent Garden who let us in provided we checked our weapons in at the door!

Viking Rig

Budget £15.

This is a really simple way to have a very different stag. All you need to create the rig is a cheap furry suede jacket and the right accessories.

Take the jacket and cut off the arms at the shoulder. Turn inside out and this is the main part of your outfit. Cut the sleeves in half at the elbow and turn inside out again. The top half becomes your furry boot covers and the bottom half sits above your wrists. Finish this off with Viking helmet, sword and axe and you're all set.

If you are close to London then Camden market is a great place for all the accessories. Charity *(thrift)* shops are the best place to get the jackets.

The Location Stag

Local vs Abroad - If budget or desire keeps you on these shores then you aren't compromising on choice, quality of talent maybe though.

The following pages list some of the potential locations but we can't cover every town or city. Local knowledge is golden so check with the lads if there is one with a cool location that was is his stomping ground. I have been on several stags with loads of local knowledge and they were always great.

This is a teaser as there is no substitute for your own research but hopefully it will give you a hatful of ideas.

Several overall websites can be quite helpful — especially to triangulate whether a place/pub/club is any good or not:

www.beerintheevening.com

www.tripadvisor.com , www.timeout.com

www.virtualtourist.com , www.nightB4.com

and because they know how to drink

www.thestudentroom.co.uk

and if you want to go more in depth:

www.lonelyplanet.com

For Those down South – 'The North'

Newcastle

	Beer

	Accommodation

	Birds

Amazing club and pub scene and loads of activities within striking distance. The Quayside is really packed on the weekends – the birds don't like Southern blokes much though.

WWW

www.visitnewcastle.com

www.nufc.co.uk

www.newcastle-falcons.co.uk

www.visitnortheastengland.com

Nottingham

   Beer

   Accommodation

🐦🐦🐦🐦🐦   Birds

The rumours are true and this is a seriously women-laden town. Clubs are plentiful and the huge student population makes for a good night out. If you are in your 30s you <u>will</u> feel old.

The centre of the town has plenty of great pubs for afternoon and early evening.

WWW

www.nottinghamcity.co.uk

www.leftlion.co.uk

www.thisisnottingham.co.uk

www.nottinghamforest.co.uk

Edinburgh

   Beer

   Accommodation

   Birds

An altogether classier stag with excellent whiskey and its fair share of clubs.

This is not a 'one festival town'. It is a beautiful and the Castle is something else and also its in the middle of the city so don't miss out on wandering up there – it's a bit of walk, but will build up your appetite.

WWW

www.edinburgh.org

www.edinburghnightsout.co.uk

www.edinburgh-festivals.com

www.vistscotland.com

[general site useful if you are visiting a smaller Scottish town].

Glasgow

 Beer

Accommodation

Birds

Excellent night out but very hit and miss on the pubs and clubs, definitely one to get local knowledge on.

You may have already glossed over Glasgow thinking of its hard nosed reputation from the 1980s (many refugees re-housed in Glasgow in the 1990s decided they were safer in their war-torn homeland and got on a plane back). Well, it still has its areas but there was a huge amount of development done when they were the European City of Culture in 1999. One of the other options is to do a two-nighter combination with Edinburgh as they are only just over an hour apart.

WWW

www.glasgow.gov.uk

www.glasgowguide.co.uk

www.theherald.co.uk

Dublin

   Beer

   Accommodation

   Birds

All I can say is top-class. Great bars, great food, great music and cheap and abundant taxis. It got expensive for a few years but the economic downturn has re-adjusted the prices to 'reasonable'

Dublin is without doubt one of the world's greatest theatres of entertainment. The Irish 'craic' is known worldwide and there's no better place to experience it than Dublin. There are mountains of activities within striking distance as well.

It is a bit of cliché to say it, but the Guiness is better in Ireland – if you ask for Guiness Extra Cold make sure you have some big lads with you otherwise you will get your ass kicked.

WWW

www.dublinevents.com

www.countydublin.com

www.visitdublin.com

Blackpool

 Beer

 Accommodation

Birds

On a decent hot day you will get 120,000+ people on the beach and along the 'Golden Mile' and there is an abundance of cheap, good quality accommodation as well to cater for the huge tourist trade.

WWW

www.blackpool.gov.uk & www.visitblackpool.com

www.blackpooltourism.com

www.blackpoolnightlife.co.uk

There are lots of other great Northern cities for nights out and you should think about your budget carefully here as you will get more for your quid *(dollar)* if you are prepared to choose a less sexy destination.

For Those up North 'The South'

Cardiff

 Beer

 Accommodation

 Birds

Cardiff is the fastest growing capital city in Europe and you can feel it. One of the lads mags voted it the UK's top night out and one of the key reasons is it's seriously compact. Within 400 metres you have casinos, bars, restaurants, and lap dancing clubs.

The Millennium Stadium also provides another interesting place to involve in the activities. I'd argue its one of the best sporting venues in the UK. Accommodation close to the centre is easy to arrange.

Added advantage from London is the intercity train which takes you straight there.

WWW

www.cardiffcityfc.co.uk

www.netcardiff.co.uk & www.bigcardiff.co.uk

www.cardiff.gov.uk

Bristol

   Beer

   Accommodation

🐦🐦🐦   Birds

Bristol was always a good party town and they have made virtually the whole of the town centre pedestrianised, which means pub-crawling is fantastic. There are two universities and countless adult education centres, which gives a student population of over 50,000. The live music is brilliant and if you can put up with the accent then the birds are ok. Avoid going during the school holidays as without the students it really feels a bit empty.

WWW

www.whatsonbristol.co.uk

www.guide2bristol.com

www.visitbristol.co.uk

London

   Beer

   Accommodation

   Birds

London has absolutely everything in abundance and it's a great jumping off point for the continent. Covent Garden and Soho are right on top of each other. There are many clubs that specially cater for stags – Bad Bobs, Salsa and Los Locos are three.

There is so much choice that you really need to sort your theme or type.

The big downside for London is drink cost – beer prices are only not expensive if you are a Parisian (£10 for a beer in central Paris). Check out happy-hours and bucket deals.

WWW

www.thisislondon.com

www.timeout.com/london

www.coventgardenlife.com

Abroad

The advent of cheap airline tickets meant you could get to stunning locations like Prague for the better side of £90 – which is still possible but tougher to do. Prior planning here will save you stacks of effort and money too. Most low-cost airlines punt *(put out)* cheap fares out 18-20 weeks in advance – the £30 a head type. Don't wait around for the £1 each way marketing gimmicks as these are always restricted to around half a dozen tickets per flight and you won't get the whole group on (unless your stag is Nobby No-Mates and there is only the four of you).

See the 'Low Cost Airlines' reviewed later in the book.

Strong Recommendation: Seriously consider using a decent stag company if you are going to venture into some of the newer destinations. Unless of course you are lucky enough to have a couple of well-organised lads to help out with the arrangements.

We have been inundated with stories of "Stags Gone Wrong" where a bunch of lads have hit a new destination with not a clue where to go and an in-built assumption that everyone will speak English – which they don't – or won't when confronted by a bunch of ill mannered piss heads *(drunks).*

Eastern Europe

Prague

 Beer

 Flights

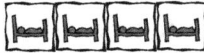 Accommodation

 Birds

OK to get to and reasonable on the beer and food – though prices have crept up in the last two years. The most stunning architecture in one of the most beautiful cities in the world – but you're interested in the beer. Czech beer is world famous and the west has truly arrived here with the full compliment of activities.

WWW

www.prague-guide.co.uk

www.pragueexperience.com

www.prague-info.co.uk

Budapest

 Beer

 Flights

 Accommodation

 Birds

Arguable the best looking women in the East and still fairly cheap on the beer and food front. This is one of the club capitals of the world too. For the more cultured of you head up to the castle they have an all you can drink wine tasting cellar.

Also the centre of the porn-filming industry – why? Hot women combined with stunning architecture Sherlock.

WWW

www.budapest.com

www.budapestsun.com

www.gotohungary.com

Riga

   Beer

   Flights

   Accommodation

🐦🐦🐦🐦   Birds

There are a million or so Latvians in Riga [about the size of Bristol] and it's a personal favourite of mine as is the only party town that has its own Bobsleigh Run. If that isn't enough excitement how about Kalashnikov shooting, or perhaps the lovely Latvian women are enough for you.

A high proportion of Riga ladies are Russian and the city has a huge 'mail order bride' business – there's a limit to what you should bring back on duty free though.

One of the best activity & party cities – would definitely go through a stag company for this one to ensure you don't get the usual amateurs that appear in a fast growing economy

www

www.virtualriga.com

www.riga-life.com , www.rigathisweek.lv

Tallinn

 Beer

 Flights

 Accommodation

 Birds

In previous editions we recommended getting in quick with Tallinn - this is the historic city that Prague was ten years back and has decent clubs and bars.

They have taken a lot from their neighbours in Finland in terms of drinking and many bars stay open until dawn. The strip clubs are good though as with any destination get a personal recommendation to avoid paying €200 for a beer – which as per most Eastern countries will set you back less than 50p.

Some of the operators offer a mock 'KGB Kidnapping' – bundled in the back of a car at gunpoint after a stack of beers....interesting.

WWW

www.tallinn.info   - very unusual virtual tour.

Vilnius

 Beer

![Flights icon] Flights   [3 hrs]

![Accommodation icon] Accommodation

 Birds

Another of the new breed which scores a five for beer purely because you can buy a round for a rugby team and still have change from your five pound note.

The activities are more limited but then you are visiting perhaps one of the newest locations on offer. Karting in winter has the added 'ice' interest and there is some decent kayaking. AK47 shooting is not for the timid.

The film industry is big here and you'll see why as the landscape and architecture is great. It was 2009 city of culture (allegedly).

WWW

www.vilnius-life.com

www.visitlithuania.net

Warsaw

 Beer

 Flights

 Accommodation

𝔶𝔶𝔶 Birds

Virtually everything built in Warsaw has been done in the last 5 decades as it was almost completely destroyed in the war. In 1980 the rebuilding of the old town led to it becoming a UNESCO World Heritage site. It's famous for is female mud-wrestling clubs, and is best visited between May and October. Be careful with January and February as the temperature can drop to −30c . The club culture caters for the 200,000 resident students so is seriously kicking. The best lagers are EB, Okocim and Zyweic and you should sample bison vodka − branded Zubrowka while you're there.

WWW

www.e-warsaw.pl

www.visitpoland.org

Russia   [the real one]

🍺🍺🍺	Beer
✈✈✈	Flights
🛏🛏🛏	Accommodation
🐦🐦🐦	Birds

Bold are we? Travel times are a little bit long but you will have a great time and the £ and $ still go a very long way. You only have to talk a few people to hear horror stories and this is definitely not the place to flaunt your TAG (even if it's a fake).

This is going to be an expensive stag as you're probably going to head to Moscow or St.Petersberg (else you will be flying on a plane with propellers).

Former Russian states are well worth a look – if you head to the Ukraine, take a local with you.

WWW

www.russia-travel.com

www.waytorussia.net

Western Europe

France

 Beer

 Flights

 Accommodation

 Birds

I'd avoid it if I were you. They don't like the English and that goes double for groups of pissed lads.

Besides, it's lazy. Make an effort please.

Amsterdam

 Beer

 Flights

 Accommodation

 Birds

A bit like Dublin in that it has for a few years clamped down a little on stags but still an absolute screamer. Hundreds of bars, good beer, legal drugs and professionally laid on prostitution + a group of lads = ability to indulge in a variety of vices in one night. June to October there are many festivals that you can jump on into.

www

www.simplyamsterdam.nl

www.amsterdamby.com

www.holland.com

Berlin

 Beer

Flights

Accommodation

Birds

Culture and excellent clubbing. Described by one of the sites below as "a teeming cauldron of debauchery" it is literally a 24hr party town. It is possible to keep going all the way through from Friday to Monday – not many cities can boast those opening hours. The arts are heavily government subsidised so if you're feeling cultural and sophisticated it's easy and cheap to fit in.

WWW

www.berlin-life.com

www.justberlin.org

+ Lonely Planet and Timeout for Berlin.

Belgium

 Beer

 Flights

 Accommodation

🐦🐦🐦 Birds

Pardon? How the heck did Belgium get in here you ask? Well, They have the best beer in the world but beware as some of the monk beers will knock your head off (15%!). Antwerp is a great night out and this and other coastal cities have the advantage of being accessible by ferry (more drinking time). Brussels can also be pretty cool and you can get some amazing packages with top-notch hotels thrown in (this is mainly because the city's corporate hotels empty out at the weekends).

Eurostar for the train fans among you have interesting packages available from them too from Kings Cross St. Pancreas station in London.

WWW

www.visitbelgium.com

+ Lonely Planet and Virtualtourist for Brussels.

Spain

 Beer

 Flights

 Accommodation

 Birds

A very nice guarantee of decent weather and the most logical of the European countries in terms of drinking habits. A nice siesta in the middle of the day (i.e. fall asleep in the sun by the beach which is only a 5 minute metro ride from the city centre after a lunchtime session) will set you up nicely for the night that will stretch to late morning the next day.

If you are into football then watching Barcelona at the Nou Camp with 98,000 Spaniards is pretty special.

If you just want drinking, fish-n-chips and SKY TV then head for the south coast chav-infested resorts – that have got surprisingly expensive recently. To be honest if you're even considering it then pick up this book and throw it our of the nearest window. After all, all these big words must be hurting your shaven head.

The USA

 Beer

 Flights

 Accommodation

 Birds

You, your stag and all his mates are minted, budget is no problem and you're off to the land of the free. You're probably going to go to the East coast unless you like spending half the stag weekend on the plane.

A few things to remind you of:

1. The legal age for drinking is 21 so just double-check you don't have any puppies along.

2. The beer tastes like cat wee (apart from some nice local beers) - choose imports.

3. The legal age of consent is 18 (unless apparently in some states where you can ask for the parents permission, then it's sixteen) – "Excuse me mate, I know you're daughter's only sixteen but do you mind?" does **not** tend to work.

4. The policemen carry guns.

5. So do many women.

6. Smokers beware – "I really need a fag" may get you some interesting results – and bans mean many clubs and pubs are smoke free – as most European cities are now too.

7. Big City Americans will not be impressed by you being British – though tell them you know David Beckham personally and you could be well in there.

8. 80% of the time they will believe you.

9. Trust me – you cannot handle a 'large' portion of food anywhere out there (you will be tempted to try as you will be off your face). You will be embarrassed like a girl as you quickly realise why many Americans haven't seen their feet since they were in high school.

10. If you visit Manhattan you may never leave – its very, very, very cool.

WWW

www.ny.com

www.newyork.com

www.nycgo.com

The Activity Stag

There are literally hundreds of centres around the UK with more cropping up all the time. A search on the net will give you plenty to choose from though buyer beware. If you can't get a personal recommendation then try and get there yourself to check out the facilities. There are some important things to watch for on the safety front.

The activities are getting pretty varied and there are some gems out there.

Take into account how many lads you are organising for. I've done stags of 7 which we've made pretty complex, but also been on ones with 20+ lads and in that case it pays not to be too over ambitious.

The market for activities has really evolved from AK47 shooting and Bobsleigh runs to white water rafting and ice karting. Try not to blow your entire budget on one novelty as it's unlikely to be fun for everyone.

Quads/Go Carts/Driving Activities

1. These may look very exciting but check out what the track is. This will vary from an awesome 'through the woods' all-terrain activity to a very poor mud ridden field.

2. Check out the engine size. The speed and excitement of a 125cc quad is eclipsed by a monster 450cc larger machine.

3. Most importantly, check out how many vehicles they have for your group. You can do the maths if you have a group of 12 and they only have 4 quads – you'll spend 2/3 of your time waiting around.

There are some seriously interesting looking activities for those with smaller groups. Tank driving has been around for a while though there are nice variations turning up (amazing how cheap you can get an ex-Ukrainian tank these days). Hovercrafts are expensive but stunning, semi-submersibles are great fun though you can't really beat fighting tough terrain in an original Land Rover Defender.

Shooting

1. There is a great choice out there so do not get stuck with piss poor air rifles that have been around for 20 years. Multi-shot cartridge guns with proper sights are common.

2. If you are going to go with shotguns/clays then check out the centre's safety record – particularly ask around their precautions for damage to shoulders/arms.

3. Archery is a good leveller as most people haven't tried it and it's good for a laugh.

4. There are more unusual items too like blowpipes.

5. Shooting activities involve very little waiting time and can be made competitive too.

6. Absolutely stick to shooting non-living things. You may think its novel to go pheasant hunting but its not clever – and you are likely to put a lot of the lads off and offend some too.

Paintball

1. This is not great if it's raining.

2. This will be much more expensive than you think as you will be going back over and over for extra paintballs at £7 a batch – especially if you are a vicious bastard.

3. Unless you have a really big group you will be lumped in with other teams, which takes a little away from the experience.

4. Beware the 'Hunt The Stag' game at the end. No one ever tells you that the best man is also the prey.

5. Nothing beats the feeling of shooting an opponent sixteen times and hearing him yelp.

6. Make sure you have some way of easily identifying the stag. A bright t-shirt to put over the overalls works really well – as is a luminous mowhawk for his helmet.

7. Really avoid the guys who bring their own guns – they may look like nerds but they will have shot you two dozen times with their Cougar Treble Hard Bastard Mark III before your single-shot pop gun has reloaded.

Other Activities

Food

This is a tough one. You can get pre-arranged meals (more practical if you have a big group) but you'll need to be pretty good with timekeeping to get there in time.

Activity Food

Themed restaurants can be a laugh. School Dinners and Medieval themes give the benefit of interesting waitresses but watch the amount of time they eat up.

Nightclubs

Getting pre-allocated tickets to a club is vital. Check to make sure that your tickets entitle you to 'Queue Jump' and don't be lazy and take the first club that the agent offers you (call me cynical but they will try and offload the tickets to the crap clubs to get the best commissions). This is definitely a time to get hold of someone who knows the clubs in the town concerned.

I won't bother recommending any as it's a personal thing but try and find a bigger one with a choice of dance floors and a variety of music.

Lap-Dancing-Clubs

Here's the thing. The spectrum of quality and worthiness of these places is very wide. They can be a laugh and who can argue with copious amounts of flesh but they can also be extremely annoying as the dancers will try and part you with your cash as fast as possible. At £20 for three minutes you can get through a serious amounts if you find it difficult to say no to 'Can I give you one?'. Try and make sure the stag gets a 'Double' so he gets the one chance in his life of seeing two tasty naked women spank each other inches from his face.

WWW

www.spearmintrhino.com

www.stringfellows.com

www.secrets-clubs.com

Strippers

Welcome to a serious lottery. A best man I spoke to during the research paid an interesting amount of wedge for a couple of 'Busty Blondes' and on the night got two very large and sweaty mingers *(aesthetically challenged ladies)*. If you are going to get a stripper then there is nothing like personal recommendation.

Yet again it's down to effort level – why not arrange to 'view the merchandise' – not down to the 'get your kecks off and lets see what you've got luv' stage but most companies can email you a respectable shot of the young lady concerned. Not too much to ask.

WWW

There are no website listings for a very good reason here – a divorce would be very costly.

Hotel

If you go for a package you may be surprised the kind of deals you can get for a few extra quid. There is no need for the Ritz here but no one is going to thank you for a fleapit with wafer thin walls and bad breakfast [Amsterdam 2003, painful no sleep memories]. Remember, most corporate hotels are empty at the weekends and depending on your group most lads are ok with sharing 3 or 4 to a room if the budget it tight.

If you are on a tight budget then budget chains like Travelodge and Travel Inn special offers are worth subscribing to on their website – they regularly have a £25-£40 per room web deals and as they sleep three (plus) it's a very low cost option.

WWW

www.laterooms.com

www.hotels.com

www.expedia.co.uk

www.kelkoo.co.uk

www.ebookers.com

Forfeits

Wherever the stag forfeits are a must. They are great fun and should always include an element of the other lads getting involved. Allocating them can be done a number of ways but here are two favourites;

1. Have a mild and tough one in each round (on the hour every hour) with the stag choosing one and the other goes to one of the lads.

2. Allocate all to the stag who can reject the worst two and allocate one to the best man.

If you go for option 2 then get all the lads to send in their choice of forfeit.

The following pages have some ideas for Mild and Strong forfeits but half the fun is thinking them up.

Mild

Hop around the whole pub/club on one foot – put your foot down then start again

Preach on a street corner for 3 minutes

Wear pants on outside of trousers for ½ hour (no covering up with your shirt!)

Get hold of a raw egg and drink it

Hand girl of lads' choice 'Talk to me' card and talk to her for a minimum of three minutes

Talk to girl of lads' choice for three minutes and pretend to be Canadian. You must finish each sentence with 'Eh' and say 'aboot' (about) at least ten times.

Monty Python 'silly walk' to the next pub/club.

Get hold of a hanky and wear it on your head for an hour like an old bloke.

You must wear shoes on your hands for 15 minutes

Strong

Drink green beer for the rest of the night (from glasses no bottles) – you need a small bottle of food colouring for this one.

Simulate sex with a road sign of the lads' choice for 3 minutes

Use a chat up line from each lad on a different woman each time (this depends on how sadistic the lads are).

You have three minutes and £20 from the whip to buy a bra off a girl and then wear it for ½ hour.

Tell ten women that you are fantastic shag.

Insert as much bread into your mouth as is possible and keep it there for 15 minutes.

The loser is blindfolded for 15 minutes. The nature of the blindfold is left to the discretion of the players.

Plunge your face into a sink full of water and scream under water. Repeat every five minutes for half an hour.

Get 5 girls to each place a Waxing strip onto one of your legs and remove (very bad version involves small strip for your nuts).

If travelling abroad, take a legal, but very embarrassing item (e.g. S&M magazine) back through customs and declare it.

Spoof

The game is legendary for allocating forfeits and rightly so as it's simple and has unlimited number of players.

The Game - Each of you has three coins and places between zero and three coins hidden in one hand. All hands into the middle and you take turns to guess the total number of coins being held – e.g. five people would mean a total somewhere between 0 and 15. You can't take a number that has already gone before. Whoever guesses correctly drops out and you go again until the loser (who gets the forfeit) is left.

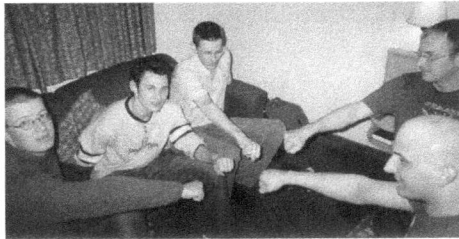

If you haven't played **'non-emotional' spoof** then it's a brilliant twist. When you go out you must say 'Thank you gentlemen spoofers, that will be me' without showing any emotion – if you do then you're back in. If there is a particularly bad forfeit on the way then the tension will build up and I guarantee you'll get people excitedly shouting "Yes!" when they drop out.

Drinking Games

Wild West

Fill 10 shot glasses - five with water and five with vodka. Mix them up and the stag has to choose five and drink them. The other lads then play spoof to drink the other five. Repeat as required.

Sevens

Everyone takes a turn to begin counting out loud one, two three, etc. when you get to a number that contains a seven or can be divided by seven then you say 'Buzz' and the game changes direction. If you pause or go wrong then you lose and down your drink.

The Drink Tower

You'll need two dice for this one. Get a stack of beer mats and a pint. The first person rolls the dice. If they get two different numbers then they place a bar mat on top of the drink and add their drink. If you throw two of the same number then you have to drink the last drink placed on the tower. However, if you throw two sixes then you have to drink the whole tower.

Case Study 1

The Stag – Charlie, 25. Left Uni a few years ago and a great chance to see his mates who have spread around the country.
The Best Man – Big brother Steve, 31.
The Lads – mainly mid 20s.
Group Size - 10
The Venue – Ultraventure Centre + Newcastle
The Type – Activity (lunch inc) + Clubbing
The Budget - £140 per head + drinks and food.

The Day

Until we are literally five minutes away from the activity centre on the border with Scotland Charlie thinks he is going to Scandinavia. We have spent the car journey letting him guess the venue and he is now convinced its Iceland.

The first part of the day is set at Ultraventure and the day's activities are shooting, quad biking and paintball.

Shooting – guns, archery and blowpipes. Plenty of practice followed by competition time. One of the lads is so hung over he misses everything and even shoots one of the other lad's targets – best laugh is definitely the blowpipes.

"Don't suck"

Quads – the choice of venue was very influenced by this activity. 450cc all terrain quads designed to clamber off-road and though dense woodland. Three circuits of a huge field littered with increasingly difficult obstacles before we are let loose in the woods. The weather is getting interesting (wet) and we're sliding all of the place – top stuff.

Eight quads mean that all the lads can tackle the obstacle course then the woods in one group.

Paintball – lots of fun and bruises. Three main games with rules, then the Hunt The Stag game with very few rules – except seven against two. Steve manages to fall out of a guard tower (it was either that or continue getting pummelled by five trigger-happy gits) and gets some nice internal bruising for his crime.

"Come here little stag.........."

"This paint tastes like crap"

The Night

Across to the hotel (The Copthorne) to shower and get changed. We head into town and find that getting a table for ten lads in a curry-house on a Saturday night even though it's early is impossible and we end up eating pizzas. Must book next time. At least it's cheap and quick and gives us more drinking time.

Head into one of the smaller clubs, which is kicking, and the music is great.

We have VIP tickets to 'Tuxedo Junction' which the club on a ship on the river. We get past the queues and head into the largest of the five clubrooms. Its time for the forfeits to come out and Dom loses the first one and spends the next 30 mins with his pants outside his trousers. Steve gets to hop round the club and has to have a few attempts as there is a rotating dance-floor. Colin has to chat-up a very large bird who almost ruins his minimum 3 minutes chat by not believing he works in France. He tries to prove this by showing her his French credit card, which she nicks, and places down her sweaty dress – Colin loses his next ½ hour trying to retrieve it.

We all roll out of the club around three in the morning and head back to the hotel. One of the benefits of a decent hotel is the 'All You Can Eat' buffet breakfast the next morning........

Left to Right - Matt, Dom, Colin, Dan M, Dan F, Steve, Tom, Charlie (Centre) and Andy (bottom)

Everyone had a cracking time, no serious injuries and some great memories.

Ultraventure is on the border between England and Scotland and around ½ hour from Newcastle.

Case Study 2

The Stag – Mike, mild mannered, shaven headed
cartoonist
The Best Man – Best mate Neil.
The Lads – mainly late 20s.
Group Size - 12
The Venue – Brighton
The Type – Activity + Curry + Lap dance + Clubbing
The Budget - £140 per head inc food.

The Day

We meet up at the activity centre, which is about
fifteen minutes outside of Brighton, just off the A23.
Most of the lads have travelled down from
Chelmsford on the train – won't do that again as
they arrive an hour late.

Shooting – very well
organised. Half the group
has archery which is
targets + two deer (can
you hit it in the head)
while the others have
rifles with a variety of
targets that drop down
once hit – with mini-clays
for the accurate.

"Crack-shot Mark"

Baby Quads – once we get over the fact that these little machines only have 125cc engines we get into the fun aspects. They only have four though, so there is quite a bit of waiting around. Sun is shining and there is tea and coffee laid on so it works well.

"Mike manages to knock every obstacle down on the way round – including the limbo bar with his head"

While we wait for the cab to take the car-less lads down to the B&B Andy goes to the boot of the car and produces a slab of cool beers. The lads are made up but the other two stag groups are pissed off they didn't think of that.

The Afternoon

A local pub round the corner from the B&B is our chance to get some serious drinking having made a quick visit to the bookies to bet on the Grand National. Neil has come up trumps with fake moustaches for everyone and we look like the cast of a 1970's German porn film. Mike the stag is kitted out with a fake tits and bum set, which gets plenty of attention from the locals.

Big Rob reckons that the girl behind the counter of the bookies is up for it (leather trousers) but we think he's talking out of his backside. We head back to the B&B to get changed for the evening.

The Night

Eleven lads in a curry house with endless pints of Tiger beer is the ideal preparation and the food is better in terms of quantity than quality.

Next stop is Pussy Cats, which is one of Brighton's smaller lap dancing clubs. Needless to say there are no pictures as cameras are seriously banned (use your imagination) but overall it proves to be a laugh. There is only one dancer on a stage, which is tiny and hidden in the corner (the stage not the lady). The ladies instead are focussed on getting private dances from the punters at £10 a time. We all have a voucher for a free dance and considering we are in there for an hour and a half and the dances last one song it's amazing we came out with any money left (you can do the math). The girls are very fit and the lads enjoy themselves. Highlight of the visit has to be the look on Mike's face when he has a 'double' bought for him and the girls spank each other just for him......

The club we end up in is excellent with two large dance floors with one garage/dance/trance and the other retro/80s music for the older lads in the group.

We roll out of the club at 3am and end up walking the two miles back to the B&B as we can't get a cab.

Note: tight legislation in Brighton and other seaside towns means minicabs cannot stop for you on the street, only black 'hackney' cabs can do that and they are pretty rare. If you are far out of the town then definitely book ahead.

Neil, Mark, Steve, Rob, Mike (centre), Andy. Rob and the lads.

Case Study 3

The Stag – Constantinos
The Best Man – Big Brother Vaz
The Lads – mainly mid to late 20s.
Group Size - 17
The Venue – Ibiza (4 nights)
The Type – Sun and serious clubbing
The Budget - £250 (flights + accommodation)

This is the kind of stag weekend that doubles as a holiday and there are plenty of takers and the big group heads off from Stanstead.

Con (with guitar) blasts out 'Love Me Tender'

The hotel is great and located in Ibiza Town, which is more traditional and well placed for San Antonio and some of the bigger clubs. It's the first week of the clubbing season with opening nights on Friday and Saturday.

Preparation is the watchword for this stag as there are no less than three dress-up evenings. The first one is the easiest with most of the lads making the effort to dress up as Elvis. Shiny shirts and quiffy wigs all round. Colin shows his Newcastle sense of humour by dressing as an Elf (Elfis) and a couple of others have gone the full hog with full-length sequinned suits.

San Antonio is a great place to kick off a night of clubbing and there are enough bars and smaller clubs to stay there all night anyway. We find a karaoke bar and murder a few of the King's tracks before we end up in an Irish pub (barmaid decides she wants to snog each Elvis) and then into Soul City, which proves to have great funky music.

The days prove to be sand, beer and football as there are plenty of games screened during the day. The second night is school uniform and the boys look really rough in their shorts.

The last night is dress-shirts with bow ties and Bermuda shorts with Con in wedding dress. He ends up unconscious after playing traffic lights with Aftershock. One of the lads pulls the tequila girl from the karaoke bar after three nights of hard work wearing down her defences.

Overall a fantastic time with stunning weather – with a group that big invariably it split into two or three groups some time in the evening which worked well as not everyone had the stamina to continue on at Pasha until 7am.

Top Tips

In this section we've tried to include ideas that will add that extra bit to the experience.....

- If its an activity weekend then put a slab of chilled beers in the boot of the car/minibus ready for the end of the day – after all the fun you will achieve hero status.

- For shooting activities take along targets made out of pictures of the stag's mother in law. You'll be amazed how the aim improves.

- Disposable cameras – you will get at least a few absolute peaches (in amongst the pictures of birds chests from the club)

- Wigs, false teeth, moustaches etc. Cheap, cheerful and a great alternative to dressing up. Gets people out of their shell too.

- Put a woman's name into an envelope for each of the lads to choose from with the target of finding (with proof) a lady with the same name – last one to reach the goal gets a serious forfeit.

- Get the stag a bespoke t-shirt done (to be worn under the 'going-out' shirt) – you should come up with a slogan that means something to the stag + embarrassing.

- If you're flying, get the smoothest-tongued of the group to convince a fit bird on the flight to approach the stag and offer to join the 'mile high club' – give him grief if he turns her down and even more when she blows him out if he's up for it.

- Everyone knows someone who knows a copper. A tough one to organise (home soil only) but a nice fake arrest during the evening will go down a treat.

- Check out a couple of things about all the lads in the group – serious allergies and any food requirements. This may seem overkill but you don't want any last minute surprises – like taking the group to an Argentinean restaurant when you have a bunch of vegetarians (been there, done that. We asked the waitress what she suggested for veggies "Another restaurant" was the short sharp reply).

- When you collect the details get mobile numbers – may seem obvious, but you can't get everything done by email. When you're on the stag remind a couple of the lads to bring their chargers with them.

- Try and hook up with the maid of honour ahead of the hen and stag – you can add little bit of extra class to the organisation to have a link between the two. This may be as simple as matching themes some time during the weekend. This makes for excellent fodder for the speeches. For example, the stag and bride on one recently were both dressed up as the Flintstones – Fred and Wilma – the pictures were a peach.

- See if anyone knows some one that is handy with websites to load up the pictures onto afterwards. If you organise this in advance then you have a chance of getting them up while everyone is still raving about the weekend.

Stag Stories

If you are a prospective groom, don't read this section..........the first four are tales personally handed over by lads who were there.

The Island

The best man is in the armed forces, which should have led to alarm bells immediately. Once unconscious after a heavy night's drinking at a southern seaside town, the groom is transferred onto a cargo plane and taken on the short hop to Gibraltar. Safely left in a barn full of straw the groom wakes up to find himself naked, apart from a single sock to cover his bits, his passport and a local banknote (equivalent to around £5). Fair play to the stag who, after cautiously making his way to the nearest town hiding in hedges and ditches, he uses the money to buy clothes off a tramp. He then hitches to the airport and blags a flight home by throwing himself on the mercy of the airline staff. They found his story very believable as he smelt of gin, pee and dog food.

Whiplash

Having gone to Amsterdam and spent the afternoon downing pints of Guinness in an Irish pub watching the rugby the lads pile into a 'show'. After a talented lady with some candles, heavy rock music announces the arrival of 'Miss Dominatrix' – 6'2" of leather-clad lovely with whips and chains. Stag is called to the stage where his humiliation begins with a dog leash round his neck and a parade around stage on hands and knees. Next comes a blindfold and handcuffing to a pole. The stag swears he hears 100+ people breath in half a second before the whip slaps across the back of his thighs – she had taken a run-up....The act finishes with Miss Dominatrix, the stag and some rather rude and functional headgear.

The Train

We've all heard of sticking the stag on the overnight train to Aberdeen but this was a nice twist. The evening was the usual fare of heavy drinking, a stripper and a pub. The stag was unconscious by eleven and his 'mates' waxed his legs and put on the train with a few quid, a pad of A4 paper and a stapler with plenty of staples. The words 'Now's your chance to be a tailor' written on the pad. Made a nice suit by all accounts – not too warm though.

The Bride's Father

Simon worked abroad when he met his fiancée and had never met her father. He knew of course that Martin ran a pub in their hometown of Bristol and would be meeting him a few weeks ahead of the wedding. His best man Pete organised, for their night out in Portsmouth for there to be a very special temporary barman in the pub that they would end up in. The plan somewhat backfired late on when the subject got onto dodgy sex and a lagered up Simon blurted out that he reckoned his bride-to-be would be up for some S&M, threesomes and giant-sized marital aids. Martin was not amused, blew his cover, broke Simon's nose and they spent the night in the A&E.

The Beard

In Sweden it is a bit of a custom for the groom to be kidnapped and whisked off somewhere for his stag night - these usually last all day and all night. Rather than the typical English stag night where you all arrange it beforehand, go out get drunk and hire a stripper, the Swedes do it differently. The groom has no idea until he gets nabbed. He might be dressed up in something crazy, and go do something fun. And then the fun starts!

This particular guy is a keen sailor and when he was kidnapped for his stag night they pasted a false "skippers-beard" on him and put him at the helm of a 60-foot yacht and let him be skipper for the day - much beer and fine food was consumed. But nothing nasty happened to him at all. In the evening when they got back on land and were getting cleaned up for the nightclub, they all had a sauna as is customary in Sweden. Imagine the groom's horror when he walked into the sauna where his naked buddies were waiting for him to see that best mate number one had no hair on his genitals. Neither did friend two, or three, or four. Herein the beard.

(from www.unclestupid.com)

Severe Sunburn

A bridegroom and his best man are recovering from severe sunburn after being dumped naked on the roadside in scorching temperatures.

The pair from south Wales were left handcuffed on the verge of the A363 after a stag night in Bournemouth.

They had been drenched in eggs, flour and tomato sauce - and as the June temperatures reached 80F (28C), their skins turned as red as the proverbial blushing bride.

The men had been subject to one last stag weekend prank by their friends, who had pulled over on the A363 Warminster bypass, near Longleat, Wiltshire.

They were held down, covered in food, and then handcuffed.

Startled motorists telephone 999 as they drove past the men, as they stumbled along the roadside.

A police car came to the rescue and took the men to the safety of Warminster police station.

A Wiltshire Police spokesman said: "Officers didn't know what to make of it.

"They were handcuffed together and very red. Some bits were redder than others - if you know what I mean!

"They must have been very sore - and I think the wedding night might be in jeopardy!"

The men were cleaned up and sent home in white paper boiler suits - normally given to prisoners whose clothes have been retained for DNA analysis - in order to spare them further embarrassment.

(from BBC Wales http://news.bbc.co.uk)

Rugby Boys (1)

The first rugby club story is the tamest of the three. Everyone knows that members of the team can be competitive but Adam and Gary carried through the whole weekend. It started with the off-road driving on the Saturday as Adam managed to shear off not just the wheel but part of the axle as well – he just had to try and beat Gaz's time and almost put the car down the hillside. The evenings drinking went off without incident but they didn't hit the sack until 4am. Sunday was clay pigeon shooting which Gary was a natural at even though he was just as hung over as everyone else. Gary hit the first three out of the trap and it was Adam's turn. The first shot was from a hide, which was enclosed from three sides and was up and over the top of the hide. Adam lined up and it must have been the adrenalin but he tracked the clay for much longer than they'd been told to, just to make sure that he'd hit it you understand. When he finally squeezed he trigger there was a shudder in the hide and the rest of the team stared in awe as they realised that he'd blown a two-foot hole in the roof.

Rugby Boys (2)

A rugby team from Manchester decided that the only place they could get a guaranteed night of raunch was Amsterdam and after an afternoon in a selection of bars they headed into the red light district. The stag was a huge prop forward called Glen and the most chauvinistic bloke you could imagine. A couple of the lads sampled the ladies behind the doors and all of them had some dope – some straight and many tried bongs. Fired up they headed to a club and Glen didn't waste any time heading straight for a very tall leggy busty blonde at the bar. The place was crawling with birds so the rest of the group didn't notice when Glen disappeared off. At about midnight one of the lads came running out of the gents and gathered everyone together. He explained that the 'bird' that he had snuck off with turned out to have some extra equipment, and was really called Yurgen....It was then they realised that Glen was gone. They headed straight back to the hotel and to Glen's room. They found him hands bound, naked clutching the bible from the side table sobbing and proclaiming his heterosexuality to his god.

Rugby Boys (3)

I wasn't going to include any really bad experiences, and then on reflection I thought I would to reinforce the fact that you need to make sure you don't overstep the line.

A rugby player on his stag night was left in agony when his pals' joke involving a pool cue went too far. Steven was strapped spread-eagled and naked to a pool table and assaulted with a pool cue.

Steven suffered serious internal injuries and had to be helped home to his wife-to-be. He later underwent emergency treatment. Police confirmed they were investigating the incident at the club reported the Daily Record.

Witnesses said they had been stunned by the ferocity of the assault. One man allegedly said: "There did not seem to be any malice. At first, it started off as a piece of fun but it very quickly got out of hand. "Steven is a big strong boy but they held him down on the pool table and it was like a whole crowd was attacking him.

"I have heard of stag night high-jinks but this takes it to a new league. It was an horrific incident."

The couple's marriage on the Saturday went ahead (just).

Agents

An industry that has now come of age. Go back five years and you'd not get much for your money, but with some companies doing over 10,000 stags a year, competition has meant that service levels have gone up a lot.

There are literally hundreds of companies that have sprung up to service this growing market. My experience with them has been very mixed though it can be a bit of a myth that you end up paying more as they often get special rates with hotels and activity centres that they use a lot.

Once you have the suggested itinerary then check out all the elements (hotel, club, activities) on the net as if you are unlucky then the agent may palm you off with either something that makes them a bit more margin or what they have left. It's worth pushing back if you are not entirely happy.

One of the key benefits is that for a small deposit you can reserve everything while you get down to your final numbers.

Note: Always check your minimum group quantities as you will always end up with less than the original list and don't overstretch yourself. Having a few mates to make up the numbers in case is a good strategy but be sensitive around this.

The Cream of the Suppliers

In selecting suppliers for this special section I went through dozens of personal recommendations. The reason there is only four here is that I wanted only to include those where either I had personally used them or I had a great report from a reliable source.

Each of the listings goes through why I chose them and why I feel they offer the best experience and overall value in their chosen area. They are all specialists and concentrate on their particular area of expertise. Enjoy, I know you will.

I struggled to single out one company at the front of long list but The Stag Company and Senor Stag seem to have cracked the simple principle that 'personal recommendation' is worth its weight in gold.

I've also thrown in an activity company – your choice for those is likely to those within driving distance so use the internet wisely – its not just there for googling 'Kylie's gold shorts' you know.

Finally I've added a 'broker' type agent as they have their place when looking for something unusual.

The Stag Company

Destination Stag

Especially - Budapest, Riga, Bratislava.
UK [Bournemouth, Brighton, Nottingham]

The Stag Company get a high percentage of their bookings from people who have already been on one of their trips – lads in their twenties and thirties tend to go on a succession of stags as all their mates get hitched in the space of a few years. Easy math – 20 lads on a very successful stag gets you quite a few repeats...

Several companies have guides – these guys decided to introduce the 'Stag Angels' – lovely ladies that will guide you around your chosen destination. Nothing gets a bunch of lads in past a club queue than a cute local lady that knows everyone.

The genius thing is that the stag company's angels are pretty and proper. Feedback from the lads on the trips is that it is great to have a cute well-dressed girl in charge. They extended recently to having stag angels in Riga and Budapest. If you're hitting Riga in the winter then seriously consider the Bobsleigh.

www.thestagcompany.com

Senor Stag

Destination Stag

Especially – Barcelona, Madrid, Seville, Valencia and the coastal resorts like Malaga.

I've chosen this agency as they are actually based in Barcelona centre. They have built a great business by constantly researching the local activities guaranteeing that they are sending you to the best places. They also get good rates because they are local and can get those illusive football tickets to the Nucamp too.

There is nothing like local knowledge and perhaps the greatest compliment that I had about these guys was from a couple of the UK based stag agencies who have used them for their own visits to Barca.

The good news is they have expanded to include Madrid, Alacante, Malaga and lots of other towns.

www.senorstag.com

Proadventure

Serious Activity Stag

Especially – if your stag is an adrenalin junkie.

Kayaking, White Water Rafting, Shooting etc.

One of the ways to get away from the distractions of unnecessary skirt chasing [you aint' going to get any when its fifteen largered up lads together] is to escape to the more remote areas of the UK.

I've chosen Proadventure as they are a centre in their own right. They are situated in Llangollen in North Wales which cleverly has fifteen pubs and bars within striking distance of the stunning countryside that is home to the fun activities.

For activity stags I'd always go with one that also does corporate events and team building – purely so that they have the funds to plough into the activities.

www.proadventure.co.uk

Chilli Sauce

Activity Stag

Especially – if you want hovercrafts, archery, rally driving.

I've mentioned that those companies that deal with corporate events can have more depth – and Chilli Sauce are proof.

They are essentially a very specialist broker working with dozens and dozens of activity suppliers across the UK and list HSBC and Barclays among their clients – which gives them buying power.

I was very impressed to see them include the Algarve as a destination – the Portuguese do sunshine coast without the need to turn it into a nineteen nineties Essex strip like some southern Spanish resorts. You can reach Faro by many low cost airlines and the food is incredible especially if the stag is into seafood.

In the first edition of Stag Night I was reluctant to include brokers as I couldn't see the added value – but the game has changed and if you're looking for activity ideas or something a little different then take a look.

www.chillisauce.co.uk

Specialist Activities

You may find that there is a particular hobby or pursuit that is big enough in the stag's life that you will go that extra mile to include a specialist activity into the weekend. This is not for everyone, but can make it really special. I've included an example here [but the only limitation here is your imagination] :

- **Favourite Football Team**

Football

How well this can work really depends on how good the chosen club is at looking after a VIP group. Getting a box allocated to you should be possible with most clubs but if your stag is a Man United fan it's a long trip up from Surrey...

In my experience the smaller the club the better you are likely to get treated but whichever one it is contact the club as early as possible. A friend of mine combined a tour of the stadium with participation in a charity event – in return for a few quid into the coffers the stag got to take a penalty against a (former) England goalkeeper who was one of his idols.

This is a good one to get a whole 'theme' around and there are endless links you can add in for the rest of the weekend – making him wear full team kit [shorts, socks but not boots as that's asking for ankle injury] for the night out is a good one – try and get the away goalkeepers strip as that is likely to be much more ugly.

The Speech

I'm not intending to give a detailed section on speeches, just a few ideas. Take a pen and pencil with you in your luggage so that you can note down anything interesting from the stag while you can still remember it. You are going to get lashed and trust me, you will forget the details by the time you sit down to finally write the speech.

The stag weekend is the ideal opportunity to find out things about the stag that you didn't know before – where else are you going to get access to most of his mates when their defences are weakened heavily by booze.

You can always resort to quoting news stories from the day the groom was born if you are stuck for something to kick off with.

The next section has a couple of the classics.

At this point I wanted to add in a niche 'best man' supplier we came across Pimp My Speech. Check it out.

www.pimpmyspeech.com - nice.

Classic Speeches

Nick what you like from these classics – the best inventions are often interpretations of proven formulas.

The Keys

You begin by telling the story of when the stag was younger and a bit of a stud. He used to have extra sets of keys cut and tell the girls that they could come by later and let themselves in. As it's his wedding day, any of them who still have a set should come and give them back. You need to prep a dozen or so girls to bring their room keys and you should have a nice metal tray for them to drop them onto as they make a nice clanking sound. Start with the young girls then add in a few mature ladies too. Add effect by asking if there are any more and you can add in one of the lads too which always gets a laugh. The most amazing version of this I have seen saw one of the lads lead in a sheep at the end with a set of keys around its neck!

The Stones

This is a very philosophical one and guaranteed to leave the older ladies sobbing but with a great laugh at the end. It's also very visual so if you are a nervous speaker this will help.

You begin with three large jars and some containers with sand, pebbles, and a large rock.

You explain that the sand represents the little things in life – good food, good music, possessions. The pebbles represent the larger things like friends and family. The rock represents your partner.

Start by pouring the sand into the first jar, adding the pebbles. You can see that the sand fits, some of the pebbles do too but there is no room for the rock.

In the second jar you put the pebbles first, then the sand, and once again there is no room for the rock.

In the third jar you start with the rock, the thing that should always come first. Then add the friends and family in the form of the pebbles. You explain that the sand should always come last as it will fit around the partner and the other pebbles that are important in your life.

You will then have a completely full jar, which represents a full life. At that point when all your mates think you have truly gone soft that you get hold of a can of beer. You then pour the beer into the full jar and everyone can see how the beer fits in between the rest of the items in the jar. You then finish with confirming that no matter how full a life is, there is always room for beer.

Movies

Here are some of movies to send the stag in the month before the weekend.

The Hangover ⑮

Simply genius. I won't spoil it for you but lets just say any film where those on the stag end up with a tiger, baby, missing teeth, an oriental hit man and Mike Tyson and one of them getting married is full of action.

I am sure that there are thousands of extra bookings in Vegas due to this film for stag weekends and we would love to hear from those that got anywhere near this much excitement.

Staggered ⑮

Stars: Martin Clunes, Michael Praed

Director: Martin Clunes

I never realised Clunes directed this but much respect to him for a classic. Neil's (Clunes) best man drugs him on his stag night and drops him onto a small Scottish Island, buck naked with no money. This is a traditional stag in that it is right on top of the wedding and the film follows his manic chase to get to the church on time. The best man is a bastard and his mother-in-law to be is a nutter. The best line in the film is right at the beginning when he meets the only inhabitant of the island and asks what the population is. "Lets just say that it recently doubled" answers the old lady.

Stag 18

Stars: Mario Van Peebles, Andrew McCarthy

If you watch this and 'Very Bad Things' you will notice that the plot is very similar – surprise stag party, stripper has an untimely death and a scramble to cover it up.

This was the first film and has a more plausible (if that's possible with this subject) storyline.

Very Bad Things 18

Stars: Cameron Diaz, Christian Slater

Hollywood version of the stag night disaster and very, very dark (read 'sick' here if you have a nervous side) indeed if you ask me. The film has little morals and is a bid of a bad boy flick with Slater doing a great job. There is a mountain of humour in it, mostly dark and Diaz is great as well.

Low Cost Airlines — The Reviews — Just to let you know what you're in for. I know you'll just go for the cheapest deal anyway...

If you are organising a stag weekend then you will undoubtedly need to involve low cost flights.

Even if the stag is in the UK then the lads travelling to it can make use of the domestic flights that are on hand.

There are some price checking sites - e.g. www.skyscanner.net but my advice is to sort out where you are going and what you are doing and then work backwards in terms of flights.

The lads will be coming from different cities so different airlines may be applicable and its also worth checking the bigger airlines too as they are having to compete and some credit cards give air-miles and may be an option for some.

Notes:

Smaller regional airports taxes are much lower than say Heathrow, Gatwick or Manchester.....

Take your own food on - two minutes invested in Pret a Manger, Starbucks, Costa or similar will spare you the [mostly] shite food on board. If you have to have a drink — have a tea. Its hard to fuck up a bag and hot water — though I have seen it done.

Value for Money vs Customer Service?

Careful, there follows a nerdy fact -

Not many people know that the lack of seat allocation on low cost airlines is the principle way they can turn planes around so many times in a day and keep costs down.

It results in the 'cattle' effect and the amazing displays of the worst of human nature as people kick and push to get the special seat on a flight that's so short the plane barely levels out before it starts its decent.....

Be realistic – you're paying the same as you would for a premiership team shirt – shut up, sit down and play with your mp3, psp or read the latest lads mag ensuring that if you are next to old people you have a 'look at the size of those' forfeit going on.....

Save your main drinking for <u>after</u> the flight – there is a temptation to get bladdered at the airport. Resist – the beer is poor quality, expensive and flying plays havoc with your alcohol tolerance.

And finally don't give the staff any crap – in the age of terrorism they can get you off the plane in a heartbeat so be a good boy.

Easyjet

www.easyjet.com

The big orange. Based out of Luton in Hertfordshire Easyjet are undoubtedly the fun airline. Great reach of destinations from Stanstead and some coverage from Gatwick too.

Good Points:

- Useful calendar mode view on the site so you can see which days are the cheapest flights
- You can select 'London All Airports' if you are travelling from the capital.
- Cabin staff seem to be quite genuine and friendly and get to wear down to earth uniforms
- Nicely bitchy adverts aimed at Ryan Air

Bad Points:

- There is only so much orange in the world
- Stelios isn't running it any more

Pricing Method.

Easyjet's fares seem to gradually increase from release – ie. Start off at around £20 then jump up in levels as the flight fills up.

Ryan Air

www.ryanair.com

Undoubtedly the most hard-hitting low cost airline out there and you can see it in the prices.

Good Points:

- They've removed the pouches on the back of the seats – this is actually a good thing as it cuts down on the crap left behind.
- You get what you pay for – a seat, although the 'standing up' fare is on its way

Bad Points:

- You get what you pay for – and caned for what you don't
- Have been on more than thirty flights with Ryanair and despite having been early to the airport on many occasions they flatly refuse to move you to an earlier flight even if its half empty
- Very poor booking process – no calendar and unless you are looking for a specific date you'll be there a while.
- Some airports they use can be a little out of the way… [check if its in the same county].

Pricing Method

Offers, offers and more offers.

Air Berlin

www.airberlin.co.uk

More than just Berlin – a decent service to all of Germany and the East and from Stanstead a wide range of Spanish and Nordic destinations.

Winning a lot of 'best budget airline' type awards.

Good Points:

- Excellent website
- Very clear charging policy with everything broken out
- Intelligent check-in where you can get onto any flight at any desk
- Has a nice feature which shows you how many seats are left on a flight if its nearly full (all of the above demonstrate German efficiency)

Bad Points:

- Fairly limited in terms of destinations from other parts of the UK

Pricing Method

Similar to Easyjet with price buckets but some special offers on the site.

BMI

www.flybmi.com

Not a bad range of destinations and definitely worth a look if you are in the Midlands.

Good Points:

- Part of the 'Star Alliance' which means they code-share and are in bed with a massive network of airlines – good for the old air miles.
- Nice cabin staff
- Good, simple and light website

Bad Points:

- Not the cheapest.

Pricing Method

Plenty of mid-range offers.

British Airways

www.ba.com

Have I turned to the wrong section or has Steve finally lost his mind.

No, honest, BA have had to shape up and with the wide range of destinations Heathrow gives them, they are worth a look – at least if you're stuck.

Good Points:

- Finally woken up to the fact that a full plane is better than five portly businessmen who don't give a monkeys about the ticket cost
- Allocated seats, food [sort of] and a general feeling that you're on a proper flight not a bus
- Airmiles partner

Bad Points:

- Uniforms still very prim and proper – still, panders to some lads fantasies of strict school marms.
- Still sometimes get the feeling of being looked down on having paid not a lot for the ticket...
- Have a tendancy to go on strike

Pricing Method

Standard fares and some decent offers.

Transavia

www.transavia.com

These guys are Dutch – for sure. Thought I'd mention it as with KLM its obvious 'Royal Dutch KLM' kinda gives it away.

Good Points

- They do Holland and not much else so they are quite good at it.
- Can select your seat online
- Allocated seating

Bad Points

- Quote "Manky old planes" from a friend who recently flew from Rotterdam – although must point out that website says *most* are modern Boeings….
- 5kg on hand baggage is a bit tight

Pricing Method

In their own words "Generally speaking, the earlier you book the lower the fare".

KLM

www.flyklm.com

Bought by Air France, (sorry, a merger) with the French airline a few years ago means a combined set of routes= quite a lot of choices....

Good Points

- Traditional airline values and an ok level of service
- Online check-in and all that good web stuff
- Regional airport coverage, although not many flights

Bad Points

- Can't ever seem to find a *really* cheap flight with these guys

Pricing Method

Some good offers when you can find them.

What about The USA I hear you Cry

American Airlines – no other US airlines comes close for flights to New York. If you are minted enough to do the US then don't muck about and choose a decent airline. Their silver planes look cool and they save on the paint.

www.americanairlines.com

But you're British I hear the gents from Eton cry so why not BA.....

Well – if I had a quid for every time I had a friend complain about BA then I'd have...... about forty quid. Last time I looked the Americans don't strike either.

If you've seen 'Up In The Air' with George Clooney (how AA managed to get Hollywood to make a 2hr AA advert I don't know) then you will know loads about them.

One exception to the mighty AA is Virgin where if you can get a good deal they are pretty good. Low cost options have crept in around the place but as ever careful that its not only the first half dozen of you that get you the good deal.

Summary

The humble stag night has changed so much over the last few years and the bar has been raised. The pressure on the best man to do a great job is immense.

Just remember the basics. Plan early, do your homework including asking local advice and don't be afraid to get some of the lads to help out.

I've been on many of these – some average and some excellent. The difference between the two wasn't the budget – it was the little things. I said it in the introduction and I'll repeat it here – the stag is supposed to enjoy most of this. Yes you need to have plenty of embarrassment and humiliation, but overall he should look back on his last blast of freedom with great, if hazy memories.

Sticking 20 beers down his neck in the first few hours so he's comatose for most of it will mess up everyone's fun.

It's your chance to shine. Don't fuck it up.

Steve

"I'm not so think as you drunk I am"

Sir J.C.Squire
Ballade of Soporific Absorption - 1931

www.ingramcontent.com/pod-product-compliance
Lightning Source LLC
Chambersburg PA
CBHW052057270326
41931CB00012B/2798

* 9 7 8 1 9 0 7 6 8 5 0 9 5 *